D0458999

The Chimpanzees I Love

SAVING

THEIR WORLD

AND OURS

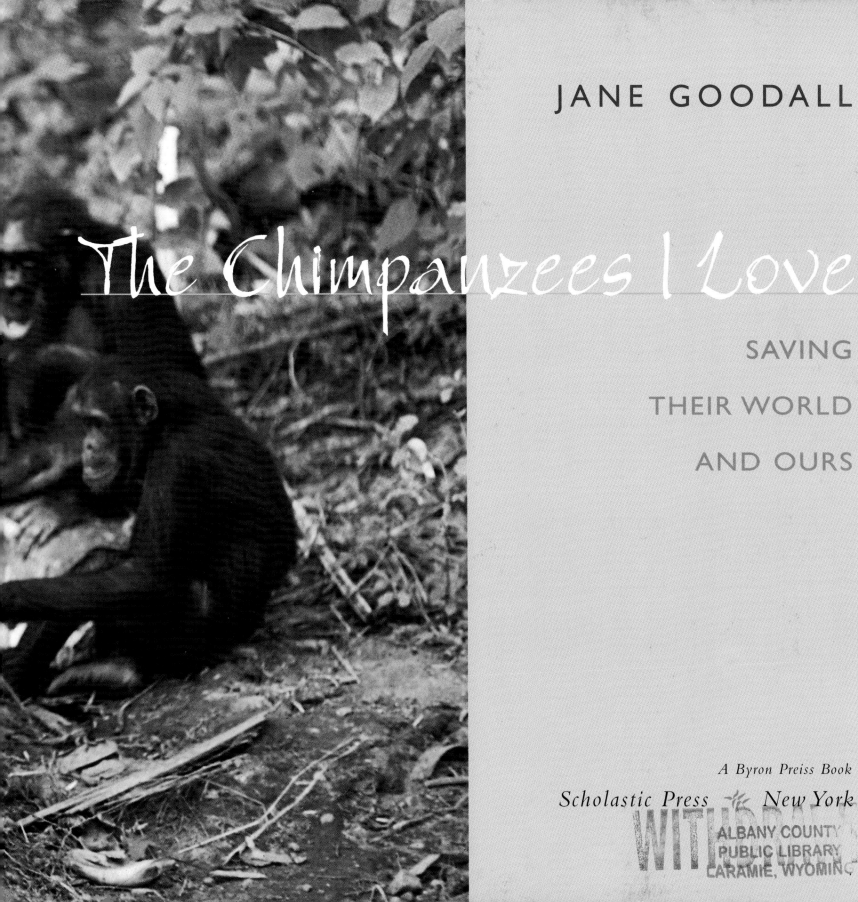

JANE GOODALL

The Chimpanzees I Love

SAVING
THEIR WORLD
AND OURS

A Byron Preiss Book

Scholastic Press New York

In memory of my mother, Vanne,
who encouraged me to always follow my dreams.
And for my sister, Judy. —J.G.

This book would not have been possible without the hard work and support of many individuals. The author would especially like to thank Lauren Thompson, Elizabeth Parisi, and Jean Feiwel at Scholastic Press; Mary Lewis and Kim Stryker at the Jane Goodall Institute; and Ruth Ashby, Valerie Cope, Erin Bosworth, Clarice Levin, Alan Schechter, Jennifer Weinberger, and Debbie Silva at Byron Preiss Visual Publications. Thanks also to Dr. Richard Wrangham of Harvard University; Dr. Tetsuro Matsuzawa of Kyoto University; Mimi Dornack of The National Geographic Society; Hedwige Boesche of the Wild Chimpanzee Foundation; Dr. Katy Gonder; Dr. Anne Pusey; Elizabeth Vinson; Michael Neugebauer; Herbert Hofer; Kristin Mosher; Tom Draper; and especially Hugo van Lawick.

Library of Congress Cataloging-in-Publication Data

Goodall, Jane, 1934-

The chimpanzees I love: saving their world and ours / Jane Goodall.— 1st ed.   p. cm.

"A Byron Preiss Visual Publications, Inc. book."

ISBN 0-439-21310-X

1. Chimpanzees—Behavior—Tanzania—Gombe Stream National Park—Juvenile literature. 2. Goodall, Jane, 1934—Juvenile literature. [1. Chimpanzees. 2. Goodall, Jane, 1934- 3. Zoologists.] I. Title.

QL737.P96 G5848 2001   599.885'092—dc21

[B]   00-047080

10 9 8 7 6 5 4 3 2 1   01 02 03 04 05

Printed in Singapore 46

First edition, October 2001

Book design by Tom Draper Design and Elizabeth B. Parisi

The text was set in 13pt. Bembo.

All of the author's proceeds from the sale of this book will be donated in support of ROOTS & SHOOTS, the international grassroots educational program of the Jane Goodall Institute; P. O. Box 14890, Silver Spring, MD 20911. Fax (301) 565-3188

For more information, please visit the Jane Goodall Institute Web site at: www.janegoodall.org.

Contents

1
Meeting
the Chimpanzees

CHIMPANZEES are more like humans than any other creature living today. When I began to study them in 1960, almost nothing was known about their behavior in the wild. In the early 1920s a scientist named Henry W. Nissen had tried to study them in west Africa, but he had learned very little. And so it was exciting when I first arrived in my study area, now the Gombe National Park in Tanzania. Ever since I was ten years old and had fallen in love with the Tarzan stories, I had dreamed of living with animals in Africa and writing books about them. And finally, when I was twenty-six years old, I was able to fulfill that dream.

My parents gave me Jubilee when I was one and a half. I still have him at my home in England, worn hairless because I carried him everywhere during my childhood.

OPPOSITE:
Gaia gazes out over her forest home.

Figaro was one of my special animal friends when I was a child.

It all began when I was a small child, loving animals of all kinds. Luckily, I had a wonderful mother who encouraged my interest. When I hid in a henhouse for four hours to find out where an egg came out, none of the family knew where I was. They searched and searched and finally called the police. Just as dusk was falling my mother saw an excited four-year-old child rushing to the house, all covered in straw. Instead of scolding me, she sat down to hear the marvelous story of how a hen lays an egg! She helped me find books about animals, and when I began talking about going to Africa when I grew up, she was the only person who did not laugh at me. Instead she told me

that if I worked hard, took advantage of opportunities, and never gave up, I would find a way. And, of course, I did!

As you read this book, you will see that chimpanzees are like us in many ways, and this makes them particularly fascinating to study. Like us, each chimp has his or her own unique personality. Chimpanzees look different from one another, too. Their brains, their blood, their DNA—the way their bodies are put together—it's all so human-like. It helps us to understand that we, like chimpanzees, are part of the great animal kingdom. Learning about chimpanzees helps us to understand ourselves better, too.

I was twenty-two years old and working in a documentary film studio in London when I received a letter from an old school friend inviting me to Kenya for a holiday. This was the opportunity I had been waiting for. I saved up enough money, working as a waitress, for a round-trip boat fare and set off. After I had been in Africa a number of months, I arranged a meeting with Dr. Louis Leakey, the famous paleontologist. Because I had learned so much about animals and Africa (even though I had never been to college), he was impressed not only by my enthusiasm but by my knowledge. He let me be part of a small group that went on a "dig" for three months each summer to look for the fossilized remains of our earliest ancestors. It was in a wild place named Olduvai Gorge, far from civilization. And he watched to see how I got on in the African bush. I passed his test, and he offered me the opportunity to go and try to learn about chimpanzees in the wild.

It took Louis a year to find funds for me to start. I had no training, I had no degree—and I was a female! Women didn't do that kind of thing in those days. But eventually he managed to get money for a six-month trial. The British authorities refused to allow a young woman into the bush on her own, but they reluctantly agreed to the expedition provided I took a companion. And it was my amazing mother who volunteered to come for the first four months. After that I was allowed to stay on without her.

From the moment I set foot on the eastern shores of Lake Tanganyika at Gombe, I felt at home. But I soon found that there was one major problem—the chimpanzees were afraid of me. Even when I was on the other side of a narrow valley, they took one look and vanished. Sometimes I despaired. I was afraid that the six months would come to an end before I had discovered anything of importance. But I found a wonderful vantage point—a rocky outcrop that I called the Peak. Every day I climbed up before dawn. I always wore the same-colored clothes and looked at the chimpanzees from afar through my binoculars, in order not to startle them. From the Peak I began to learn more and more about chimpanzees and their way of life. Everything that I saw I jotted into a little field notebook which I wrote out, in a journal, every evening.

In 1962 I was joined by Dutch photographer and filmmaker Hugo van Lawick. And, as the work increased,

Here I am with Louis Leakey in Kenya, 1958. It was Leakey who gave me the opportunity to study chimpanzees in the wild.

we employed more people to help. That meant that observations could continue even when I had to go to Cambridge University to work for my Ph.D. degree. Today most of the daily records (on baboons as well as chimpanzees) are taken by a team of Tanzanian field staff from the small villages that surround the national park. They follow a different chimpanzee each day and record his or her behavior. Gradually we have built up a collection of unique life histories and family histories. There are two co-directors of the research, one Tanzanian and one British, and at any one time there are three or four graduate students studying different aspects of behavior.

We expect that the research at Gombe will continue indefinitely into the future. We are still learning new things. As I write this, Flo's daughter Fifi, who was a little infant when I began the study, is about forty years old and has just had her eighth infant. She could easily live another ten to fifteen years.

Young chimpanzees are very curious. Fifi watches as I drink tea on the veranda of my tent.

I shall never forget the excitement and wonder of my first months at Gombe. The forests are home to all sorts of animals, and gradually I got to know them. I met many troops of monkeys: baboons and red colobus, vervet, redtail, and blue monkeys. Sometimes I startled a bushbuck with its chestnut coat, or a bustling reddish-colored bush pig. There were a couple of small herds of forest buffalo—I tried to avoid them after being charged and chased up a tree by two bulls! I learned to identify countless fascinating birds, ranging from the tiny sunbirds to the huge and secretive Verreaux eagle owl. Some have brilliant colors; many have beautiful songs.

There were two or three crocodiles in the lake, and monitor lizards, chameleons, and geckos. I saw all kinds of frogs and toads, and so many snakes—some poisonous, including the deadly green and black mambas and the feared Storms water cobras, which kill quite a few fishermen when they get caught in their nets. Sometimes I met a huge python. And, of course, there were all the thousands of species of insects, including fantastic butterflies and moths, as well as the less pleasing tsetse flies and malaria-carrying mosquitoes.

ABOVE: Green mambas can kill you with their venom. But unlike black mambas, they are not at all aggressive. Many poisonous snakes live in the Gombe National Park.

LEFT: We have been studying the baboons of Gombe since 1967.

As I became more and more familiar with my beautiful new world, I also learned more and more about the chimps. I observed how they wandered about in small, always changing groups, calling back and forth across the valleys. Sometimes I saw two groups join and feed together in a tree. I watched as they charged about in excitement, sometimes hitting one another, sometimes embracing. I watched them make sleeping beds or nests up in the trees in the evening by bending branches over a firm foundation, then bending the ends back over again. I climbed into some of these nests and found that they were strong and comfortable.

The chimps mostly traveled from place to place on the ground. Like the other great apes, chimpanzees are knuckle walkers, which means that although they walk on the soles of their feet, like we do, they also walk on the backs of the middle joints of their fingers. Sometimes I saw a chimp walking upright for a short distance—when he or she wanted to look over tall grass, when carrying fruits in both hands, or when it was raining. It seems that chimps don't like putting their hands on the ground when it is cold and wet. After an outbreak of polio, two males, each of whom had lost the use of one arm, learned

Hugo van Lawick came
to Gombe to film and
photograph chimpanzees
for the National
Geographic Society.
We watch as Flo grooms
adolescent son Faben.
Fifi is on the right.

OPPOSITE:
Chimpanzees have
gathered to feed on
new shoots in this tree.

to walk long distances completely upright to keep their limp hands from trailing on the ground.

Chimps spend a lot of time feeding and resting in the trees. Their feet are more like human hands to look at, with the big toe acting like a thumb. This makes it easy for them to hold onto branches when climbing. Like the other apes, chimps can swing hand over hand (this is known as brachiating) from branch to branch. We can swing, too, because our shoulder joints are made the same way. But our fingers are not long or strong enough for us to do it for long distances.

I began to learn about the chimps' diet. I saw them eating fruits of many kinds, and leaves, flowers, seeds, nuts, buds, pith, and stems. After watching them feed, I collected specimens of the tree or plant, which my mother put in plant presses to dry so that they could be identified later.

Juvenile chimpanzees
often play in the
branches, swinging
and dangling.

OPPOSITE:
I reach out to touch a
chimpanzee's hand.

Gremlin eats
termites she has caught
using a grass tool.

One day—in October 1960—I saw something really amazing. It was just after the rainy season had begun. I was walking through tall, wet grass when I saw a dark shape hunched over the golden-red earth of a termite mound. Carefully I moved closer and peered through the undergrowth. It was a male chimpanzee—and he was using a grass stem as a tool. He pushed the stem carefully into one of the passages leading into the nest and waited a moment. Then he withdrew it and picked off the insects with his lips and crunched them up. Sometimes he picked a leafy stem and stripped off the leaves so that it would fit into the narrow opening. He was not only using grass stems as tools—he was actually *making* tools. This was a really exciting observation for, up until then, it had been thought that only human beings could use and make tools.

Another important day, at about the same time, was when I saw chimpanzees eating meat. A male, a female, and a young chimpanzee were making a meal of a baby bushpig carcass. A few months later I saw chimpanzees actually hunting. Their prey was a young red colobus monkey, separated from its troop. The chimpanzees showed real cooperation as

Infant Flint watches intently as his mother, Flo, fishes for termites. This is how they learn the different tool-using cultures of their community.

17

David Greybeard was the
first Gombe chimpanzee
to lose his fear of the
strange white ape that
had appeared in his
territory—he became
almost like a friend.

they surrounded the monkey while one of them raced up the tree to make the kill. Then they all shared the meat. Before these observations, it was thought that chimpanzees were vegetarian.

When the National Geographic Society heard about termite fishing, and about hunting and meat eating, they agreed to give me a grant so that I could carry on with the research.

By this time I had learned to recognize some of the chimpanzees—and then I gave them names. It was not thought scientific, at that time, to give names to research subjects—I should have referred to them by numbers. But I had always named my animal friends and I saw no reason to treat the chimpanzees differently. Today, most field biologists name the animals they study.

The first chimpanzee who learned to trust me was one I named David Greybeard. He came to my camp for the ripe red fruit of an oil nut palm and found—and took—some bananas. I began to leave bananas out for him, and gradually other chimpanzees followed him to this new food source: Goliath and William, and then old Flo and her family, and many others. After about a year, I was able to get quite close to many of the chimps when I came upon them in the forest. And, once I knew them apart, I started to understand their complex society.

Fifi clutches a bushbuck that had been killed by baboons. Amazingly, she stole it from them, eventually sharing meat with the other chimps.

2

The Chimpanzee Community

THE COMMUNITY that I gradually got to know at Gombe was made up, at that time, of more than fifty individuals. There were about fourteen adult males, slightly more adult females, and a collection of adolescents, juveniles, and infants. We now know that in some areas, communities may be as large as eighty individuals. Within a community all the individuals know one another, but there are some who do their best to avoid each other, some who meet only occasionally, and some who spend a lot of time together and are real friends. This is not at all like a

> *"There is a great deal in chimpanzee relationships to remind us of our own behavior. More, perhaps, than many of us would like to admit."*

troop of monkeys, for instance, where all the members stay together almost all the time for traveling and feeding and sleeping.

A chimpanzee mother and her dependent children, up to the age of seven or eight years, are always together. Most days they meet up with other members of their community for a while, but they also spend time away from other chimpanzees, sleeping and traveling on their own. Sometimes many members of the community join one another in large excited gatherings, usually when an especially delicious food ripens in one part of their range.

Within the community the chimpanzees, for the most part, have relaxed and friendly relations. Male chimpanzees are very sociable and enjoy one another's company. Sometimes they travel around in all-male groups. But every so often a male leaves his companions and travels on his own, or with a female or a group of females and young. It was not until I had been studying them long enough to realize who was related to whom, that I

really began to understand chimpanzees' social life.

Very close relationships develop between mothers and their grown offspring and, often, between siblings. Brothers, in particular, sometimes become very close friends and allies as they grow up. They continue to spend some time with their mothers and families throughout their lives. The same is true for daughters, unless they decide to transfer into a neighboring community, in which case they will probably never see their families again. We still don't know why some females make this choice.

In chimpanzee society the various individuals are arranged in a dominance hierarchy, or pecking order. I found that Goliath, David Greybeard's friend, was the

Like her mother, Flo, Fifi is a very good mother. Here she is with offspring Ferdinand, Faustino, and Fanni.

OPPOSITE:
When they were young, Fifi and Olly's daughter, Gilka, were good friends who loved to play together.

boss or alpha. JB ranked number two, then came Hugh, and Hugo, and on down the ranks. I noticed that the adult males were able to dominate all females. The females seemed to have their own ranking order, though it was usually not very clear. Flo was obviously the highest ranked. Her friend, old Olly, ranked lowest.

Goliath was not the biggest of the males, nor was he the most aggressive. But he had a fearless nature, and he worked hard to stay on top. Male chimpanzees challenge each other by performing dramatic charging displays.

Mike learned to use noisy kerosene cans in his charging displays. Males were so intimidated that Mike, initially low ranking, became the top or alpha male.

OPPOSITE:
Goliath was the top-ranking male when I first arrived in Gombe.

They hurtle across the ground, stamping and slapping, swaying or dragging branches, picking up and hurling stones. Those with the most frequent or imaginative displays are likely to rise high in the dominance hierarchy. Goliath had a very fast and impressive charging display. But in 1964 he lost his position to Mike. At first Mike was very low-ranking, but he was determined to change that. When he was in camp, he learned to use empty four-gallon kerosene cans in his displays. Again and again I watched him gather up two or even three cans and charge toward a group of chimps, hitting and kicking the cans ahead of him. Even Goliath rushed out of the way. And then when Mike stopped, the others hurried to pay their respects to him. We never saw him actually fighting, but he took over the top position in just four months!

Mike reigned for six years, by which time he looked old—he was probably about forty-five years old—and he lost his position to the younger, heavier, and very aggressive Humphrey. Every male who has made it to the top has done so in a different way, and I have written their stories in some of my other books. After Humphrey came Figan, then Goblin, Wilkie, Freud, and Frodo, who is alpha now (February 2001).

Chimpanzees within a community seldom fight really seriously. Most of their squabbles are settled by threatening postures and gestures. They wave their arms and swagger upright with bristling hair, giving loud barking calls. The lower-ranked individuals give way, and fights are avoided. And often, after aggression, the victim approaches the aggressor and crouches submissively, making whimpering calls or screaming. Usually the victim is reassured with a gentle pat on the back, or a kiss or embrace. In this way, peace is restored.

When chimps do fight, it usually looks and sounds much worse than it is, as one or both scream loudly. Aggressors hit, stamp on, or drag their victims, but they rarely bite and their fights seldom result in severe wounding. Females fight each other most often over food or to defend their young. Males fight much more often than females, and their fiercest fights are when they are competing for social dominance.

OPPOSITE:
Male chimpanzees at Gombe charge and scream with excitement.

Here Fifi is attacking Gilka as play becomes aggressive. Such fights do not lead to serious wounds.

We also see fighting between members of different communities. This aggression is the most severe and brutal of all. Adult males frequently patrol the boundaries of their territory, and if they encounter a "stranger"—a chimpanzee from another community—they may give chase. If the victim is caught, he or she is subjected to a terrible gang attack. These strangers, usually adult females, very often die of their wounds. Only adolescent females are not attacked. Instead, the patrolling males try to lead them back into the heart of their own community range. During one four-year period we watched as the males of one community attacked the adult males and females of a smaller, neighboring community, one by one, and left them to die of their wounds. It was a kind of war. It did not end until the smaller community was destroyed—all except the adolescent females.

When a grown chimpanzee attacks, the victim can be badly hurt.

I was very sad and shocked when I found that the chimpanzees, just like us, have a dark side to their nature. We used to think that only humans engaged in war, but I found that chimpanzees sometimes show warlike behavior, too. It was terrible to watch when a group of chimps brutally attacked an individual. You might wonder why we did not try to defend the victims. In fact, chimpanzees are so much stronger than us, and they become so violent when roused, that there was nothing we could do. We did try to help the wounded victims afterward.

Chimpanzees are like humans in so many ways, but obviously there are many differences, too. Perhaps the most significant difference is that we—and only we—have developed a sophisticated spoken language. Only with a language of words can you discuss things, make plans for the distant future, teach about objects or events that are not present, and bounce ideas back and forth in a group.

Chimps do communicate with sounds, of course. They have many calls—at least thirty-four we can identify—and they all mean different things. There are small friendly grunts, angry barking sounds, the soft whimpers of distress. And there are frightened or angry screams, loud wailing alarm calls (a frightening sound in the forest), and the pant-hoot that chimps use to communicate over distance. Each individual has his or her own distinct voice, so when you hear a pant-hoot you know who is calling. This is how scattered community members keep in contact.

Chimpanzees also communicate with facial expressions, gestures, and body postures—just as we do. A low-ranking individual may greet a superior male with

LEFT: Chimpanzees have many expressions. His grin means that Mike is feeling nervous.

ABOVE: Chimpanzees can communicate by means of calls, gestures, postures, and facial expressions.

soft grunts and by crouching in front of him, sometimes holding out a hand. An upright swagger, with hair bristling, is a threat. Touching is very important. Frightened chimps reach out to touch or hug each other. Friendly individuals may kiss or embrace or hold hands. A pouting face means distress; a huge grin with teeth showing means fear. They smile and laugh with their lower teeth showing.

Chimpanzees may spend more than an hour grooming each other, moving their fingers gently through each other's hair, cleaning the skin. This is very soothing and is an important part of friendly behavior. Mothers calm their infants with grooming and spend hours grooming with grown-up offspring. Grooming is especially important between adult males, as they need to help one another to protect their joint territory.

Grooming is a very
important social activity.
It strengthens friendships
and calms nervous or
excited individuals.

OPPOSITE:
Every individual
has his or her own
distinctive pant-hoot that
is recognized by other
chimpanzees throughout
the community.

I shall never forget the day when David Greybeard allowed me to groom him. An adult male chimpanzee, living in the wild, trusted me so much that he let me groom him. I decided later it was a mistake. It is not good to make direct contact with the chimpanzees, for many reasons. We want to observe their natural behavior and not interfere. If they get too familiar, they can be dangerous, as chimps are so much stronger than humans. They might catch an infectious disease from us, or we from them. But some of those early interactions were so special. It was a wonderful reward for hours of patience and determination.

Scientists used to think that only humans have emotions, such as happiness and sadness, anger, fear, and

It was a proud moment when David Greybeard, a wild male, first allowed me to groom him.

despair. Now many researchers are studying animal emotions. As with humans, often you can tell a lot about the mood of a chimpanzee by watching the expression on his or her face.

I had one wonderful communication with David Greybeard as I followed him in the forest. When he sat close to a little stream, I sat nearby. I saw a ripe red fruit of an oil nut palm lying on the ground. Chimps love these fruits. I held it out to him on my palm. He turned his head away. I held it closer. He looked into my eyes, took the nut, dropped it, then very gently held my hand. It is the way chimpanzees reassure one another. He didn't want the nut, but he knew I meant well. It was a communication, between human and chimpanzee, that could be understood without words. It was a moment I shall remember all my life. I can still close my eyes and feel the soft, warm skin of his fingers pressing mine.

Here Figan pulls on my hand trying to persuade me to play with him.

3
Mothers and Babies

Faustino

I HAVE LEARNED so much about the importance of family life from Fifi and her old mother, Flo. (Their family is known as the F family, since all its members have names beginning with F.) I first knew Fifi when she was a little infant in 1961. Ten years later, Fifi gave birth for the first time. She made a big night nest and settled down. In the morning little Freud, as we called the baby, was in the nest with her.

In the wild most females know how to care for their babies because they have watched other mothers and, unless they were the last born in a family, have been able to play with, groom, and carry their younger brothers and sisters. That was certainly true for Fifi. Flo had been a wonderful

OPPOSITE:
Fanni gazes down
at Fax.

mother: attentive, protective, affectionate, and playful. She also supported Fifi when she and her brothers got into trouble with other chimps. Fifi had learned much about maternal behavior from watching Flo with her young brother, little Flint, in 1964. She had been absolutely fascinated by the infant and spent hours sitting close to Flo, wanting to groom or play with him. When Flint was five months old, Flo sometimes let her carry him when the family traveled.

Fifi's own infant, Freud, was born in 1971. Fifi was an excellent mother from the start. When Freud nuzzled her breast, searching for the nipple and making tiny *hoo, hoo* sounds, she helped him so that he could suckle. She always cradled him with one hand as she traveled until he was strong enough to cling on by himself.

Other mothers are less concerned—mothers like Passion and Patti. Passion was rather harsh and cold in her treatment of her infants, though she got better with each successive birth. Patti simply had no idea how to care for her firstborn, who died as a result. She was not much better with her second, but he survived in spite of his mother's lack of skill. By the time she gave birth for the fifth time Patti was a very good mother.

Fifi cradles Freud.

OPPOSITE:
Flo was a wonderful mother to Fifi and Flint. Fifi was utterly fascinated by her infant brother Flint. Here she is kissing him.

"Chimpanzees are more like us than any other living beings."

I loved watching Fifi and Freud. She cared for him so well. For five years Freud suckled and shared his mother's nest at night. At first he always clung to her belly when she traveled, but at five months he began to ride more and more often on her back. He took his first tottering steps and climbed his first branches at the same time, always under the watchful eye of his mother.

Fifi, like her mother Flo, was sociable and spent a lot of time with other members of the community. Once he had learned to walk and climb, Freud had a lot of opportunities to play with others, including adult males. He learned a lot during play about the characters of other infants, and also about the characters of their mothers. If he upset a child with a high-ranking mother, he would be quickly scolded, and then Fifi would get involved, hurrying over to defend Freud.

Freud also learned a lot when he was amusing himself, leaping about in the branches or playing with

Young chimpanzees spend hours playing together when their mothers meet.

OPPOSITE:
Two Gombe families spend time together. From left to right: Ferdinand, Gaia, Gremlin, Galahad, Fifi, and Faustino.

various objects—as a human child plays with toys. He learned from experience. He learned what was frightening and how to behave in all sorts of different situations. When Freud made a mistake he was sometimes punished. If, for example, he went too close to a male who was in a bad mood he sometimes got threatened, even hit. And he learned, too, by watching and then imitating what others did, especially his mother, Fifi. He ate what she ate, in the same way. He practiced using grass tools when she was fishing for termites, sticks when she was catching ants, leaves when she was drinking from a rain-filled hollow in a tree, and so on.

Freud, like all infants, was very upset when Fifi began to wean him—when she would not let him suckle or ride on her back. He would rush off screaming and hitting the ground. Then Fifi followed and held him tight. "You can't have milk or ride on my back anymore," she seemed to be telling him. "But I love you just as much." By the time Freud was five years old and had accepted the new rules, his little brother was born. Freud, like almost all older brothers and sisters, was fascinated by the new baby, Frodo. As soon as Fifi allowed it, Freud began to play with, groom,

Like human children, young chimpanzees love to play.

and carry Frodo. Because Freud stayed with Fifi even after weaning, he was a wonderful playmate for the new infant and a role model, too. Frodo watched everything his big brother did, and often tried to do the same. Because of this, he did a lot of things at a younger age than Freud had.

It was fascinating to see how the members of this family helped one another. Fifi, like many other individuals, became higher-ranking as she got older. And so, when Freud began to challenge the females of his community, he got the better of all those who ranked lower than Fifi—because she always rushed to help him. And then, as he grew older, he in turn helped Fifi until she became the

top-ranking female. He and Fifi both helped Frodo in his battles, and as more offspring were born they all helped one another. The youngest family members had even more older siblings (brothers and sisters) to help them.

When Freud was ten years old he began to challenge the adult males. Gradually he worked his way up to the top position by the time he was twenty-two. He ruled the community for four years. Then, when Freud was very sick during an epidemic of a horrible skin disease, his top position was seized by his younger brother, Frodo. (Fifi was also very sick, losing all her hair. And her seventh infant, Fred, was so sick that he died.)

These two young chimps are good friends.

Throughout the forty years of the study at Gombe, we have known some wonderful chimpanzee characters, a few of whom I have described in this book. And we have observed some amazing and often rather sad events. When Flo died she must have been over fifty years old. She was shrunken, her hair sparse, her teeth worn to the gums. She avoided big groups and traveled mostly on her own, accompanied only by eight-year-old Flint. He was with his mother when she died, and although he was easily old enough to fend for himself, it seemed as though he couldn't cope with life without her. He became more and

more depressed. He didn't want to eat; he didn't want to interact with other chimps. In this state he fell sick and died six weeks after losing Flo. I think he died of grief.

And then there is my very favorite story. When Miff died, she left a sole surviving child, three-and-a-quarter-year-old Mel. Infant chimps depend on milk for at least three years. And Mel was not only very young, but sickly, too. We were sure he would die. To our amazement, a twelve-year-old male adolescent, Spindle, adopted him. He waited for Mel in travel and let the infant ride on his back and sleep with him at night. He shared his food when Mel

Flint was the first wild chimpanzee whose development we were able to document from birth until his death.

OPPOSITE:
Flo was an affectionate and playful mother. Here she tickles Flint, who is laughing.

43

begged, and he even rushed to move Mel to safety if the infant got too close to big males about to start their wild charging displays. This is something a mother does until her child is old enough to get out of the way itself. It is important because during their charging displays the big males sometimes pick up and throw, or drag, infants who are in their way. They don't seem to notice them. This was particularly brave of Spindle because he was at that age when adolescent males have to be more and more cautious of the big males, who see them as potential rivals. Usually they keep well out of the way when their heroes are socially excited. Spindle actually got hit on several occasions when he rescued Mel. But he always did it.

Spindle saved Mel's life. It is interesting to know that Spindle lost his mother, the ancient Sprout, during the epidemic that killed Mel's mother. At twelve years old, a chimp doesn't need his mother to survive. But if he gets beaten up, or gets hurt or scared in any way, he will go and spend time with his mother, if she is alive. Perhaps the death of Sprout left a space in Spindle's heart. Perhaps his close contact with small Mel, who depended on him so much, helped to fill that space. I don't suppose we shall ever know.

Small Mel was left alone and defenseless after the death of his mother—until Spindle adopted him and saved his life.

OPPOSITE:
When Winkle died, nine-year-old Wunda adopted her infant brother, Wolfi. She carried him, shared her nest with him, and protected him.

4

A Day in the Forest

FOR WILD CHIMPANZEES, every day
is different from the one before. But, to give you a feeling
of life in the forest, we will follow Gremlin for a day.
I have chosen Gremlin because she is my favorite living
female. She is the third female whom we know has given
birth to twins. Gremlin has four children on this day in
1999. The eldest is adolescent Galahad, then comes
seven-year-old daughter Gaia, and the twins, both female,
whom we have named Gold, or Goldie, and Glitta. I
invite you to come with me into the forest and follow
Gremlin and her family and meet her friends and
acquaintances.

OPPOSITE:
Gremlin and her twin
daughters, Goldie and
Glitta.

47

We are up above the calm water of Lake Tanganyika, sitting quietly. Gradually the moonlight changes to the gray light of dawn. High above us there is a rustling of leaves. That is where, the night before, we left Gremlin and her children. All over Gombe, chimpanzees are beginning to wake up, moving sleepily in their leafy beds. And all over Africa, wherever there are chimps, they will be getting ready to start a new day.

As it gets lighter, Gremlin moves again and there is a sound like falling water and the thudding of heavier things landing on the ground. Chimpanzees, unlike gorillas, never dirty their nests unless they are very sick. Then Gremlin, still lying, idly grooms Glitta, who has moved close to suckle. There are more rustling sounds and Gaia swings from her little nest nearby, climbs over to her mother Gremlin, and, holding up her arm, asks to be groomed. Gremlin sits up, yawns, then the two groom each other. Glitta climbs into sister Gaia's lap. Glitta's twin, Goldie, the more adventurous of the two, climbs carefully to join her older brother, Galahad, in his nest, about ten feet away.

Soon Goldie returns. Gremlin gathers her two babies, climbs down, and moves off through the undergrowth, both twins riding on her back. Gaia follows, and we crawl and wriggle after them. Galahad is moving in the trees above. Soon Gremlin climbs a tree of ripe figs. And there, feeding overhead, we find Gremlin's brother, Gimble. They all give soft, happy-sounding grunts, pleased to see one another. Gaia runs to kiss Gimble's head and he touches her back in a gentle greeting. Galahad gives his uncle a quick groom.

The chimps feed contentedly. A pair of robin chats sing their beautiful duet. A little squirrel climbs a tree, spiraling around the trunk. And there are glorious butterflies flitting near the forest floor. After an hour, there are rustling sounds in the undergrowth and two adult males appear: Frodo, who is currently the alpha male, and Goblin, Gremlin's eldest brother. When Gremlin and her children see them, they give loud, excited pant-hoots. Galahad rushes down to greet them. But before he gets there, they start to perform magnificent charging displays, rushing around on the ground below the tree, dragging branches, and hurling rocks. Galahad, screaming, quickly climbs back up the tree. Frodo, then Goblin, hit and kick the wide buttresses of a huge forest tree, making a drumming sound. Then they calm down. Their display of strength is over, and they climb to feed.

OPPOSITE: Goldie, with her distinctive white beard, rests contentedly on Gremlin's back. Glitta is hanging on below.

"The forest is for me a temple, a cathedral of tree canopies and dancing light."

About fifteen minutes later, we hear more rustling sounds and the cracking of sticks as more chimps arrive. This time it is our friend Fifi and her three youngest children, the boys Faustino and Ferdinand and infant daughter Flirt. Fifi sits below the tree, looking up. She gives soft greeting grunts when she meets Goblin's eye. The boys rush up the tree to greet the big males. Then Faustino starts a chasing game with Galahad in the branches, and Ferdinand goes to play with Gaia. Goldie joins in and they are both very gentle with her. Fifi climbs up to groom with Goblin, Flirt asleep in her arms. There are soft chuckles of chimp laughter as the youngsters play together. Glitta stays close to her mother and carefully investigates little holes in the tree. Once we see her poking at a trail of ants with a twig and stamping at them as they race around on the branch.

As the day warms up, the adults come down, one by one, and stretch out on the ground. Gremlin, with the twins and Fifi's boys, stays in the tree. It is very peaceful. The only excitement is when a baboon troop passes nearby and, for ten minutes or so, Gaia goes off to play with two juvenile male baboons. They chase each other, crashing from branch

Faustino and Ferdinand
pause while feeding
on leaves.

to branch, as Gaia tries to pull their tails. Then they follow their troop away, and Gaia climbs to play with Glitta.

An hour later they all move off together. Suddenly we hear the birdlike calls of red colobus monkeys above us in the canopy. The chimps are excited. They reach out and touch one another, their hair bristling. Then they climb and start to hunt. It is Frodo, the great hunter, who succeeds in snatching a tiny baby monkey from its mother. He kills it with a quick bite on its neck. The others gather around to beg. Frodo is not generous, but most of them get something. Fifi grabs quite a big piece and moves away to enjoy it, chewing each mouthful slowly along with a handful of leaves. Her young children beg from her. Gremlin, burdened with her twins, stays away. Gaia whimpers as she begs from Frodo, but she gets nothing.

When the meat is finished the group breaks up. The older males move off in one direction. Gremlin and Fifi with their younger offspring travel together. Presently Gremlin notices an underground bees' nest. She breaks off a thick stick to enlarge the opening, then, ignoring the angry bees, reaches in and scoops out a handful of

Fifi with Flirt,
her eighth offspring.

honeycomb. The twins, whimpering, bury their faces in their mother's hair. Fifi rushes over to get her share. They move away from the bees to enjoy this delicious feast. The twins lick the honey from Gremlin's hand. Gaia cautiously approaches the nest and bravely grabs a little bit, wildly hitting at the bees with her free hand. Ferdinand and Flirt share with Fifi.

Soon after this Fifi sets off, following Ferdinand, who has heard the pant-hoots of his brother Faustino and wants to join him.

Suddenly Galahad appears, crashing through the branches above, disrupting the feast. Gremlin gathers up

her babies and they all move off. They pause to bend and drink from the clear water of a small, fast-running stream. Then, in the soft light of evening, they climb for their last meal of the day: bright yellow blossoms.

And then it is time for sleep. Gremlin moves into a thickly leaved tree nearby. She chooses two branches and bends smaller branches over them. Last, she folds over the leafy ends of the branches so that her springy treetop bed is soft and comfortable. She picks a few more leafy twigs and arranges them as a pillow. Then she settles for the night and the twins suckle. Gaia makes her own nest nearby. Galahad continues eating for a

TOP: **Gaia dips a handful of leaves she has gathered into the hollow of a tree. She is trying to retrieve water with her home-made sponge.**

Gaia makes a comfortable nest high in the treetops.

while. Then he, too, makes his nest and lies down.

Throughout the forests of Africa, the chimpanzees have settled down to sleep after a long, busy day. In some places it will be raining, and they will be miserable and cold. But the chimps in Gombe have two months before their wet season begins.

Just as we are about to leave Gremlin to go home, we hear, from the deep forest, the pant-hoot of a single male.

We recognize the voice of Goblin. Gremlin and Galahad call out in reply. Gaia joins in, and the twins give their tiny startled *oo oo oo* sounds. From farther away, other chimps join in, their voices swelling into a musical chorus. Then they fall silent as the dusk gives way to the tropical night. We pick our way down the mountain slope, using our flashlights, to the thatched metal house on the beach that is my home at Gombe.

Some of the sunsets over Lake Tanganyika are glorious, especially in the wet season.

5

The Mind of the Chimpanzee

ANIMALS ARE much smarter than scientists used to think. I was told at school (fifty years ago) that only human beings have personalities, can think and reason, feel pain, or have emotions. Luckily, as a child, I had spent hours learning about animal behavior from my dog, Rusty—so I knew none of that was true!

The more we have learned about chimpanzees, the clearer it is that they have brains very like ours and can, in fact, do many things that we used to think only humans could do. I've described how the Gombe chimps use grass

stems and twigs to fish termites from their nests. The chimps also use long smooth sticks to catch vicious biting army ants. They use crumpled leaves to soak up water from hollows in trees that they cannot reach with their lips, then suck the homemade sponge. They wipe dirt from their bodies with leaf napkins. They use stout sticks to open up holes in trees to get at birds' nests or honey and as clubs to intimidate one another or other animals. They pick up and throw rocks as missiles. In other parts of Africa, chimps have different tool-using behaviors. For instance, in west Africa and parts of central Africa, they use two stones, a hammer and an anvil, to crack open nuts. It seems that infant chimps learn these behaviors by watching the adults, and then imitating and practicing what they have seen. So the chimps have their own primitive culture.

Many scientists are finding out more about the chimpanzee mind from tests in captive situations. For example, chimps will go and find sticks to pull in food that

Figan sucks rainwater from a sponge tool made of crumpled leaves.

OPPOSITE:
Chimpanzees in Guinea use a pair of stones as a hammer and anvil to crack open oil palm nuts.

"How many times I have wished that I could look out onto the world through the eyes, with the mind, of a chimpanzee. One such minute would be worth a lifetime of research."

has been placed outside the cage, beyond their reach. They can join two short sticks together to make one long tool. They have excellent memories—after eleven years' separation, a female named Washoe recognized the two humans who had brought her up. A chimp can plan what he or she is going to do. Often I've watched a chimp wake up, scratch himself slowly, gaze around in different directions, then suddenly get up, walk over to a clump of grass, carefully

select a stem, trim it, and then travel quite a long way to a termite mound that was out of sight when he made his tool.

Chimpanzees can be taught to do many of the things that we do, such as riding bicycles and sewing. Some love to draw or paint. Chimps can also recognize themselves in mirrors. But they cannot learn to speak words because their vocal cords are different. Two scientists, the Hayeses, brought up a little chimp named Vicky and tried to teach her to talk. After eight years she could say only four words, and only people who knew her could understand even those.

The Gardners had another idea. They got an infant chimpanzee, named her Washoe, and began teaching her American Sign Language (ASL) as used by deaf people. Then other infant chimps were taught this language. Chimps can learn 300 signs or more. They can also invent signs. The chimp Lucy, wanting a Brazil nut but not knowing its name, used two signs she knew and asked for a "rock berry." A fizzy soda became "listen drink," a duck on a pond, "water bird," and a piece of celery, "pipe food." Washoe's adopted son learned fifty-eight signs from Washoe and three other signing chimps by the time he

was eight years old. He was never taught these signs by humans. Other chimps have been taught computer "languages" and can punch out quite complicated sentences. These experiments have taught us, and continue to teach us, more and more about the chimpanzee mind.

OPPOSITE: **Ai is famous in Japan for her computer skills. She does some tasks more quickly than high school children. She has done better than me, too.**

Ai has been learning language skills at Kyoto University since 1978. Her six-month-old infant, Ayumu, will learn to stack blocks just like a human child.

Zoos are improving
gradually, but thousands
of chimpanzees around
the world spend their lives
in barren cement-floored
cages with nothing to do.

Unfortunately chimpanzees, so like us in many ways, are often very badly treated in many captive situations. Chimpanzees were first brought to Europe from Africa in the middle of the seventeenth century. People were amazed by these humanlike creatures. They dressed them up and taught them tricks.

Since then we have often treated chimpanzees like slaves, shooting their mothers in Africa, shipping them around the world, caging them in zoos, training them to perform in movies and circuses and advertisements, selling them as pets, and imprisoning them in medical research laboratories. Some chimps become famous. J. Fred Muggs starred on TV's *Today* show for years and was known by millions of viewers. What they didn't know was that whenever one J. Fred Muggs got too big and strong for the show, he was replaced by a younger one.

A young male called Ham was sent up into space. He was shot up in a Mercury Redstone rocket in January 1961, and because he survived the ordeal (he was terrified), it was decided that it was safe for the first human astronauts. Ham was taught his routine by receiving an electric shock every time he pressed the wrong button. Often circus chimps are taught, right at the start of their training, that instant obedience is the way to avoid a beating. The beatings are given when the trainer and chimp are on their own, so no one sees. It is the same for other animals—and for many of those used in movies and other forms of entertainment.

Infant chimpanzees are adorable and, for the first two or three years, are gentle and easy to handle. People buy them and treat them like human children. But as they grow older they become more and more difficult. They are, after all, chimpanzees, and they want to behave like

I visit La Vielle in her dark cage in the Point-Noire zoo. I am showing her *The Chimpanzee Family Book.*

chimpanzees. They resent discipline. They can—and do—bite. And by the time they are six years old they are already as strong as a human male. What will happen to them then? Zoos don't want them, for they have not been able to learn chimpanzee social behavior and they do not mix well with others of their kind. Often they end up in medical research labs.

It is because their bodies are so like ours that scientists use chimps to try to find out more about human diseases and how to cure and prevent them. Chimpanzees can be infected with almost all human diseases. Hundreds have been used (with no success) in AIDS research. The virus stays alive in their blood, but they do not show the symptoms. It is very unfair that, even though chimpanzees are being used to try to help humans, they are almost

Forty-three-year-old Susie has been in show business for more than thirty years.

never given decent places to live. Hundreds of them are shut up in 5′ x 5′ x 7′ bare, steel-barred prisons, all alone, bored, and uncomfortable. Measure out this space and imagine having to live in it your whole life. (Many closets are much bigger!)

I shall never forget the first time I looked into the eyes of an adult male chimpanzee in one of these labs. For more than ten years he had been living in his tiny prison.

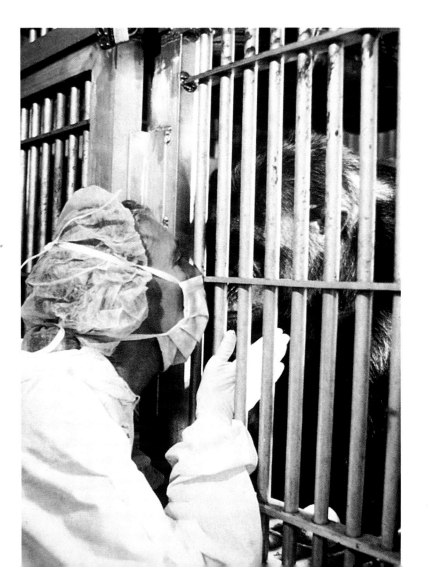

The sides, floor, and ceiling were made of thick steel bars. There was a car tire on the floor. His name, I read on the door, was JoJo. He lived at the end of a row of five cages, lined up along a bare wall. Opposite were five more cages. At either end of the room was a metal door. There was no window. JoJo could not touch any of his fellow prisoners—only the ends of his fingers fitted between the bars. He had been born in an African forest, and for the first couple of years he lived in a world of greens and browns, leaves and vines, butterflies and birds. Always his mother had been close to comfort him, until the day when she was shot and he was snatched from her dead or dying body. The young chimpanzee was shipped away from his forest world to the cold, bleak existence of a North American research lab. JoJo was not angry, just grateful that I had stopped by him. He groomed my fingers, where the ridges of my cuticles showed through the surgical gloves I had to wear. Then he looked into my eyes and with one gentle finger reached to touch the tear that rolled down into my mask.

In the United States, several hundred chimpanzees have been declared "surplus"—they are no longer needed for medical research. Animal welfare groups are trying to

La Veille spent years alone in a Congolese zoo. We were able to move her to our Tchimpounga sanctuary and introduce her to other chimpanzees.

OPPOSITE:
JoJo and I touch through the bars of his prison cage in a research lab.

raise the money to build them sanctuaries so that they can end their lives with grass and trees, sunshine and companionship. Some lucky ones—including JoJo—have already been freed from their laboratory prisons. Many others are waiting.

Zoos are getting better, but there are still many chimps in small concrete and metal cages with no soft ground and nothing to occupy them. Good zoos keep their chimpanzees in groups and provide them with all kinds of stimulating things to do, different things each day, so that they don't get bored. Many zoos now have artificial termite mounds. Chimps use sticks or straws to poke into holes for honey or other foods. These innovations make a world of difference.

6
Protecting the Chimpanzees

CHIMPANZEES live in the forested areas of west and central Africa. In some places, where there is a lot of rain, these are thick tropical rain forests. In other places there are strips of dense forest along the rivers, with wood-land and even open grassland in between. The chimpanzees usually cross open ground in groups, traveling without stopping until they reach the safety of the trees again. Chimpanzees can survive in quite dry areas, but there they have very big home ranges, for they must travel widely to get food. Like the other African great apes, the gorillas and bonobos, they are disappearing very fast. One hundred years ago we think there were about two million chimpanzees in Africa; now there may be no more than 150,000. They are already extinct in four of the twenty-five countries where they once lived. There are more chimpanzees in the great Congo basin than anywhere else—but that is where they are disappearing the fastest. They are disappearing for various reasons:

1. All over Africa, their forest homes are being destroyed as human populations grow and need ever more land for their crops and for their homes, and ever more wood for making charcoal or for firewood.

2. In many places chimpanzees are caught in snares set for bushpigs or antelopes. Snares were once made of vines, but now hunters use wire cable. Often the chimps are strong enough to break the wire, but they cannot get the noose off. Some die; others lose a hand or a foot, after months of agony.

3. There are still dealers who are trying to smuggle chimpanzees out of Africa for the live animal trade. Mothers are shot so that hunters can steal their infants for entertainment or medical research. Many individuals die in the forest (including adult males who rush to the rescue and are shot) in order for one infant to reach its destination alive. The dealers pay the hunters only a few dollars while they themselves can sell an infant chimp for $2,000 or more.

4. The greatest threat to chimpanzees in the great Congo basin is commercial hunting for food. Local tribes, like the Pygmies, have lived in harmony with the forest and its animals for hundreds of years. Now logging companies have made roads deep into the heart of the last remaining forests. Hunters ride the trucks to the end of the road and shoot everything—chimps, gorillas, bonobos, elephants, antelopes—even quite small birds. The meat is smoked or even loaded fresh onto the trucks and taken for sale in the big towns. The trouble is that so many people living there prefer the taste of meat from wild animals, and they will pay more for it than for that from domestic animals. If this trade (known as the "bushmeat" trade) cannot be stopped, there will soon be no animals left.

Little Jay just after we confiscated him, with the help of the government, in the Congo. Graziella (left) offered to try to nurse him back to health. He was the first infant I saw, with my own eyes, tied up for sale in an African market.

There are many people and organizations trying to help protect chimpanzees and their forests, but the problems are very hard to solve. Most of the people destroying the forests are very poor. They can't afford to buy food from elsewhere, so they cut down more trees for their farms and shoot or snare more animals for food. Because the soil needs the shelter of the trees in the tropics, the people are soon struggling to survive in a desert-like place. So they cut down more trees. And the bushmeat trade has become a very big money-making operation, with many high-up government officials involved. We shall not give up until solutions have been found.

These days it is not enough for a scientist just to study animals in the wild. It is necessary for us to try to protect them and their environment, as well. The Jane Goodall Institute was founded in the United States in 1977. At first we just raised money to keep the research at Gombe going, but gradually we realized we had to do more. In 1960, when I first got to Gombe, you could go for miles and miles along the shore of Lake Tanganyika and you would see forests rolling down to the water's edge. Today it is different. The thirty square miles of the Gombe National Park still look the same. But outside the park the trees have all disappeared, cut down by the continually growing human population, swelled by hundreds of refugees from Burundi and eastern Congo. The once-lush slopes are becoming more desert-like as the soil is washed down into the lake with every rainstorm.

Soon we had to face a very important question: How could we save the approximately one hundred chimpanzees left in the Gombe forests, when people outside the park, and the environment they depend on, are suffering? It was this question that led to a major program that seeks to improve the lives of the people living around Gombe National Park. In thirty-three villages in the area there are tree nurseries. Bare slopes are being planted, wells for clean water are being built, women are getting new opportunities for education, children are learning about conservation. Things are getting better for these

The hills above Gombe, once so green and lush (left), are now bare (right).

A caretaker at Tchimpounga sanctuary in Congo-Brazzaville feeds a group of hungry orphans. In the background, adults who have already had breakfast watch with interest.

"Every individual matters. Every individual has a role to play. Every individual makes a difference. And we have a choice: What sort of difference do we want to make?"

people, and they understand that the forests of Gombe are important. More and more of these programs are starting up around conservation areas.

We are also trying to care for many infant chimps whose mothers have been shot for food. There is not much meat on these infants, so they are often sold as pets or to attract customers to a hotel or bar. As this is illegal in most countries, we can persuade government officials to confiscate these infants. Then we try to nurse them back to health, give them lots of love, and care for them in sanctuaries. They cannot go back to the forest—the wild chimps would attack them, or they would wander into a village and be hurt or hurt someone, for they have lost their fear of people. So we have to care for them for the rest of their lives. The Jane Goodall Institute has sanctuaries in Congo-Brazzaville, Uganda, and Kenya, and is building one in South Africa. You could help us care for our orphan chimps by becoming a Chimp Guardian. You can find out how to do this by contacting the Institute.

It is easy to feel depressed when you think about all the problems in the world. When I think of all that humans have done to spoil our planet during the sixty-six years of my own life, I feel very sad—and ashamed of our own species. But I am full of hope, too. That is why I started a program called Roots & Shoots. Why is it called Roots & Shoots? Roots make a firm foundation; shoots seem small, but to reach to the light they can break apart brick walls. Imagine the brick walls are all the bad things that we humans have done to the planet—to the environment, to animals, to one another. But hundreds and thousands of roots and shoots—young people like you—around the globe can break through and make the world a better place for all living things.

Roots & Shoots is the education program of the Jane Goodall Institute. You can check it out on the Web site or call or write to our mailing address. I'd love you to be part of it. It began in Tanzania, but now there are groups in more than fifty countries. Every group chooses at least one hands-on activity in each of three areas to show care and concern: 1) for animals, including dogs, cats, cows, and so on; 2) for the human community; 3) for the environment we all share. The projects you choose depend on whether you live in the inner city or in a rural area, in the United States or Africa or China or wherever. People of all ages, from kindergarten to college, have joined Roots & Shoots. It's growing very fast.

The most important message I have for you is that you, as an individual, can make a difference every day of your life. And you can choose what sort of difference you want to make. People ask me why I have so much hope for the future when things often seem so grim.

I'll tell you. First, it's because human beings have very clever minds, and recently scientists and industry and the general public have been getting together to find ways to do things that will be less harmful for the environment. Second, it's because nature is amazingly forgiving—even when we humans have really spoiled a place that was once beautiful, it can regenerate if we give it a chance and perhaps some help. And animal species that are almost extinct can, if we work hard to protect them, start to multiply again. Third, I feel hopeful because of all the wonderful people I meet, the people who tackle impossible tasks—and succeed.

And finally, I have hope for the future because of the energy and commitment and persistence of young people around the globe. I get so excited when I hear what all the Roots & Shoots groups are doing to make the world a better place. Everywhere more and more people have begun to understand that their own lives *do* matter, that we are all here for a purpose, and we can each of us make a difference. We shall not let the chimpanzees become extinct in Africa, and we shall not let them go on being cruelly treated in captivity. Chimpanzees are more like us than we ever used to think. They make us realize that there is not, after all, a sharp line dividing humans from the rest of the animal kingdom. So we think of all animals with new respect and with greater compassion.

As a small child I never dreamed how my life would be changed—and made richer—by the time I have spent living with the chimpanzees of Gombe. I hope your life, too, will be the richer for knowing about them, and I hope you will be inspired, as I was, to do all you can to make the world a better place for all living things.

Jou-Jou has been caged alone in a Congolese zoo. He reaches to touch me, desperate for contact.

FACTS AND RESOURCES

The chimpanzee, whose scientific name is *Pan troglodytes* (pan trog-low-*die*-tees), is a primate. The primate family includes galagos or bushbabies, lemurs, marmosets, monkeys, apes, and humans. Apes are humanlike creatures with no tails. There are the so-called lesser apes—the gibbons and siamangs—and the great apes—orangutans in Asia, chimpanzees, bonobos (formerly called pygmy chimpanzees), and gorillas in Africa. Humans are another kind of great ape. Today monkeys are smaller than apes, but there were huge monkeys and lemurs in prehistoric times.

Scientists believe that primates are descended from small, insect-eating mammals that lived about sixty-five million years ago. Gradually some of them grew larger, and they became more intelligent. Apes and humans descended from a common ancestor sometime within the last fifteen to twenty million years.

Chimpanzees are more like us than any other creature alive today. The structure of their DNA differs from ours by only just over one percent. Humans can receive blood transfusions from chimpanzee donors. And chimpanzees can catch or be given all our infectious diseases—which is why some scientists use them in medical research. In fact, biologically, chimpanzees are more closely related to humans than they are to gorillas.

THE PRIMATE FAMILY

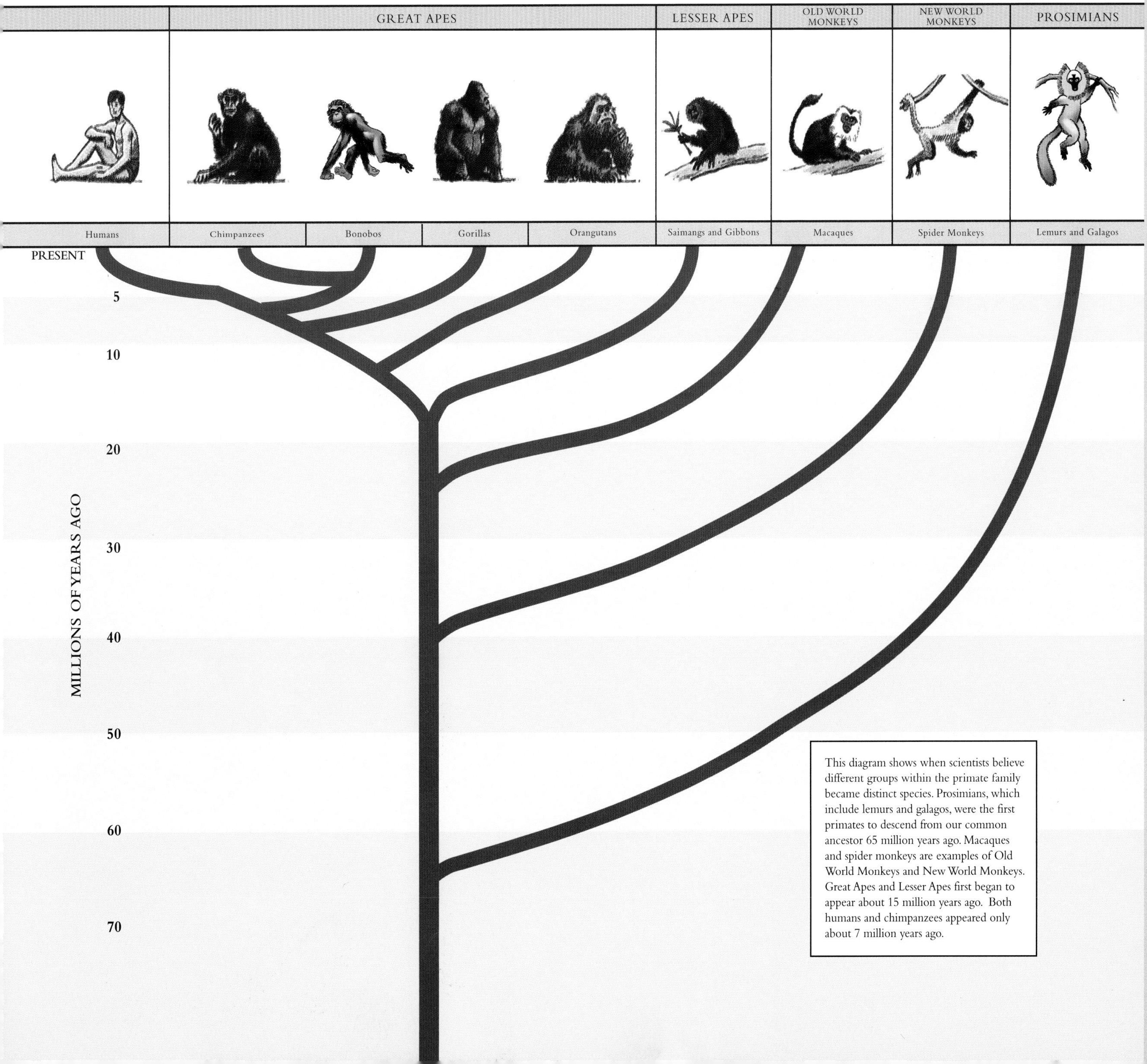

	GREAT APES				LESSER APES	OLD WORLD MONKEYS	NEW WORLD MONKEYS	PROSIMIANS
Humans	Chimpanzees	Bonobos	Gorillas	Orangutans	Saimangs and Gibbons	Macaques	Spider Monkeys	Lemurs and Galagos

PRESENT

MILLIONS OF YEARS AGO

5

10

20

30

40

50

60

70

This diagram shows when scientists believe different groups within the primate family became distinct species. Prosimians, which include lemurs and galagos, were the first primates to descend from our common ancestor 65 million years ago. Macaques and spider monkeys are examples of Old World Monkeys and New World Monkeys. Great Apes and Lesser Apes first began to appear about 15 million years ago. Both humans and chimpanzees appeared only about 7 million years ago.

Chimpanzee Facts

- A fully grown male chimpanzee at Gombe is about 4 feet tall and weighs up to 115 pounds. The female is about as tall, but she is lighter, seldom weighing more than 85 pounds.

- In west and central Africa the chimpanzees are a little bigger and heavier. Often they are heavier in captivity, too, at least when they are well fed and given medicine. This is not surprising, as they have much less exercise than when they live in the wild.

- Chimpanzees in the wild seldom live longer than fifty years, though some captive individuals have lived more than sixty years.

- A female chimpanzee in the wild raises two to three offspring, on average. But she may raise as many as eight or nine.

Chimpanzee Habitats

Chimpanzees are found in twenty-one African countries, from the west coast of the continent to as far east as western Uganda, Rwanda, Burundi, and Tanzania. Chimps live in the greatest concentrations in the rain forest areas along the equator. Due to the fast-paced destruction of these rain forests, as well as other pressures, chimpanzees are considered an endangered species.

The Gombe Stream Research Center is located on the eastern shore of Lake Tanganyika, in Tanzania.

CHIMPANZEE RANGE

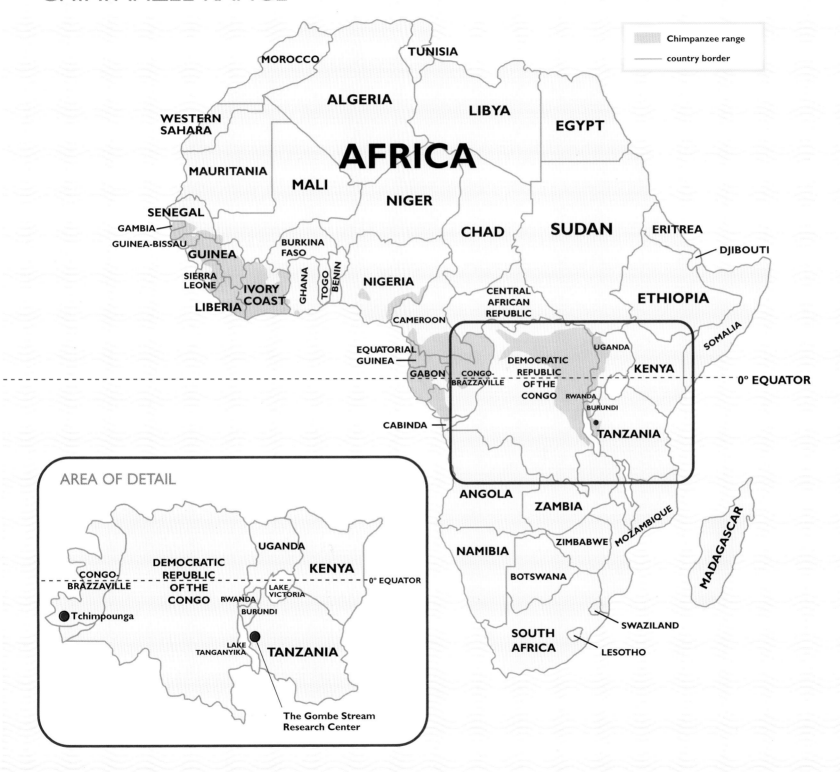

MOROCCO
TUNISIA
ALGERIA
LIBYA
EGYPT
WESTERN SAHARA

AFRICA

MAURITANIA
MALI
NIGER
CHAD
SUDAN
ERITREA
SENEGAL
GAMBIA
GUINEA-BISSAU
GUINEA
BURKINA FASO
DJIBOUTI
SIERRA LEONE
IVORY COAST
GHANA
TOGO
BENIN
NIGERIA
LIBERIA
CAMEROON
CENTRAL AFRICAN REPUBLIC
ETHIOPIA
EQUATORIAL GUINEA
GABON
CONGO-BRAZZAVILLE
DEMOCRATIC REPUBLIC OF THE CONGO
UGANDA
KENYA
SOMALIA
RWANDA
BURUNDI
0° EQUATOR
CABINDA
TANZANIA
ANGOLA
ZAMBIA
MOZAMBIQUE
MADAGASCAR
NAMIBIA
ZIMBABWE
BOTSWANA
SWAZILAND
SOUTH AFRICA
LESOTHO

AREA OF DETAIL

CONGO-BRAZZAVILLE
DEMOCRATIC REPUBLIC OF THE CONGO
UGANDA
KENYA
0° EQUATOR
RWANDA
LAKE VICTORIA
BURUNDI
Tchimpounga
LAKE TANGANYIKA
TANZANIA

The Gombe Stream Research Center

The Jane Goodall Institute

The Jane Goodall Institute for Wildlife Research, Education, and Conservation was founded in 1977. Over the years, this not-for-profit organization has expanded its mission from providing support for field research on chimpanzees and protection of chimpanzee populations to combining efforts in education, community development, conservation, and humanitarianism to make the world a better place for all living beings. The Institute runs several programs, ranging from TACARE, a reforestation and conservation education project in western Tanzania, to ChimpanZoo, an international program dedicated to the study of chimpanzees in zoos and other captive settings and to enriching their lives.

Roots & Shoots

Roots & Shoots is an environmental and humanitarian education program especially for young people, founded by Jane Goodall in 1991. In schools, community-based clubs, and other youth groups, Roots & Shoots members participate in projects that promote care and concern for all animals, the environment, and the human community, and experience directly how their actions can make a difference in the world around them. Roots & Shoots groups have formed in all fifty of the United States and in more than fifty countries around the world, creating a global network of young people, from preschool through college, committed to positive action. Through Roots & Shoots, Dr. Goodall welcomes youth everywhere to join in her vital work.

For more information, contact:

Roots & Shoots, The Jane Goodall Institute
P. O. Box 14890, Silver Spring, MD 20911
Fax (301) 565-3188

Or visit the Jane Goodall Institute Web site:
www.janegoodall.org

Other Books by Jane Goodall

FOR YOUNG PEOPLE

My Life with the Chimpanzees
New York: Simon and Schuster, 1988.
Revised edition, Minstrel Books, 1996.

The Chimpanzee Family Book
Ridgefield, CT: The Jane Goodall Institute, 1989.

With Love
New York: North-South Books, 1994.

Dr. White
New York: North-South Books, 1999.

The Eagle and the Wren
New York: North-South Books, 2000.

FOR OLDER READERS AND ADULTS

In the Shadow of Man
Boston: Houghton Mifflin, 1971.
Revised paperback edition, 1988.

Through a Window
Boston: Houghton Mifflin, 1990.

Visions of Caliban: On Chimpanzees and People
With Dale Peterson. New York: Houghton Mifflin, 1993.

Jane Goodall: 40 Years at Gombe
Produced in association with the Jane Goodall Institute.
New York: Stewart, Tabori and Chang, 1999.

Reason for Hope: A Spiritual Journey
New York: Time Warner Books, 1999.
Paperback edition, New York: Warner Books, 2000.

Africa in My Blood: An Autobiography in Letters (vol. 1)
Edited by Dale Peterson. Boston: Houghton Mifflin, 2000.

Beyond Innocence: An Autobiography in Letters (vol. 2)
Edited by Dale Peterson. Boston: Houghton Mifflin, 2001.

Video and Audio Documentaries

Among the Wild Chimpanzees (video)
National Geographic Society, 1984.

Chimps, So Like Us (video)
An HBO film, 1990.

My Life with the Chimpanzees (video and audio)
National Geographic Society, 1990.

Reason for Hope (video)
KTCA, PBS special, 1999.

All books, audios, and videos available from JGI.
www.janegoodall.org

Picture Credits

Front jacket and cover (main photo): © Michael Neugebauer, E-Mail: mine@netway.at; **(top, left):** Kristin Mosher/Danita Delimont, Agent; **(top, right):** Michael Nichols/NGS Image Collection. **Back jacket and cover:** Ken Regan/Camera 5. **Half-title page:** © Michael Neugebauer, E-Mail: mine@netway.at. **Title page:** Hugo van Lawick/NGS Image Collection. **Contents page:** © Michael Neugebauer, E-Mail: mine@netway.at. **Page 6:** © Michael Neugebauer, E-Mail: mine@netway.at. **Pages 7–8:** © Eric Joseph, courtesy the Goodall family. **Page 9:** © Joan Travis. **Page 10:** Hugo van Lawick/NGS Image Collection. **Page 11, left:** © Craig Lovell/CORBIS; **right:** © Brian Vikander/CORBIS. **Page 12:** Hugo van Lawick. **Page 13:** Vanne Goodall/NGS Image Collection. **Page 14:** Michael Nichols/NGS Image Collection. **Page 15:** © Stephen Patch, courtesy The Jane Goodall Institute. **Page 16:** Jane Goodall. **Page 17:** Hugo van Lawick/NGS Image Collection. **Page 18:** Jane Goodall/NGS Image Collection. **Page 19:** Michael Nichols/NGS Image Collection. **Page 20:** Courtesy The Jane Goodall Institute. **Page 21:** Kristin Mosher/Danita Delimont, Agent. **Page 22:** Hugo van Lawick/NGS Image Collection. **Page 23:** © Gerry Ellis/GerryEllis.com. **Pages 24–26:** Hugo van Lawick. **Page 27:** Hugo van Lawick/NGS Image Collection. **Page 28:** Hugo Van Lawick. **Page 29, both:** Hugo Van Lawick. **Page 30:** © Stephen Patch, courtesy The Jane Goodall Institute. **Page 31:** Jane Goodall. **Pages 32–33:** Hugo van Lawick/NGS Image Collection. **Page 34:** © Michael Neugebauer, E-Mail: mine@netway.at. **Page 35:** © Gerry Ellis/GerryEllis.com. **Page 36:** Hugo van Lawick/NGS Image Collection. **Page 37:** Jane Goodall. **Page 38:** © Michael Neugebauer, E-Mail: mine@netway.at. **Page 39:** Jane Goodall. **Page 40:** Hugo van Lawick. **Page 41, both:** Michael Nichols/NGS Image Collection. **Page 42:** Hugo van Lawick/NGS Image Collection. **Page 43:** Hugo van Lawick. **Page 44:** © Michael Neugebauer, E-Mail: mine@netway.at. **Page 45:** Jane Goodall. **Page 46:** Kristin Mosher/Danita Delimont, Agent. **Page 47:** © Gerry Ellis/GerryEllis.com. **Pages 49–52:** Kristin Mosher/Danita Delimont, Agent. **Pages 53–54:** Michael Nichols/NGS. Image Collection. **Page 55:** © Eric Joseph, courtesy the Goodall family. **Page 56:** Hugo van Lawick/NGS Image Collection. **Page 57:** Tetsuro Matsuzawa. **Page 58:** Nobuyuki Kawai and Tetsuro Matsuzawa. **Page 59:** Tetsuro Matsuzawa. **Page 60:** Courtesy The Jane Goodall Institute. **Page 61, both:** Michael Nichols/NGS Image Collection. **Page 62:** Courtesy The Jane Goodall Institute. **Page 63:** Michael Nichols/NGS Image Collection. **Page 64:** Jane Goodall. **Page 65:** Courtesy The Jane Goodall Institute. **Page 67:** © Michael Nichols. **Page 68, both:** Jane Goodall. **Pages 69–70:** Michael Nichols/NGS Image Collection. **Page 71:** David Grubbs/Billings Gazette, Montana. **Page 72:** Michael Nichols/NGS Image Collection. **Page 74:** Hugo van Lawick/NGS Image Collection. **Page 75:** Diagram by Debbie Silva. **Page 76:** Kristin Mosher/Danita Delimont, Agent. **Page 77:** Map by Debbie Silva. **Page 78:** Michael Nichols/NGS Image Collection. **Page 79:** © Michael Neugebauer, E-Mail: mine@netway.at.

ADDITIONAL CAPTIONS

Front jacket and cover (main photo): I sit with Sophie, an orphan who lives at Sweetwaters Sanctuary in Kenya. **Half-title page:** Sophie and I. **Title page:** I have gained Flo's trust so much that she allows her infant, Flint, to reach out and touch my hand. **Contents page:** I visit with a group of Sweetwaters Sanctuary chimps in Kenya, 1995. Max has his hand on my shoulder. **Page 74:** Figan allows me to tickle him. Chimp laughter is quite like human laughter. **Page 76:** Curious about the world around her, Flirt pauses during her climb up a young tree. **Page 78:** As I travel around the world, I meet thousands of young people concerned about animals and the future of the environment. **Page 79:** Galahad and I.